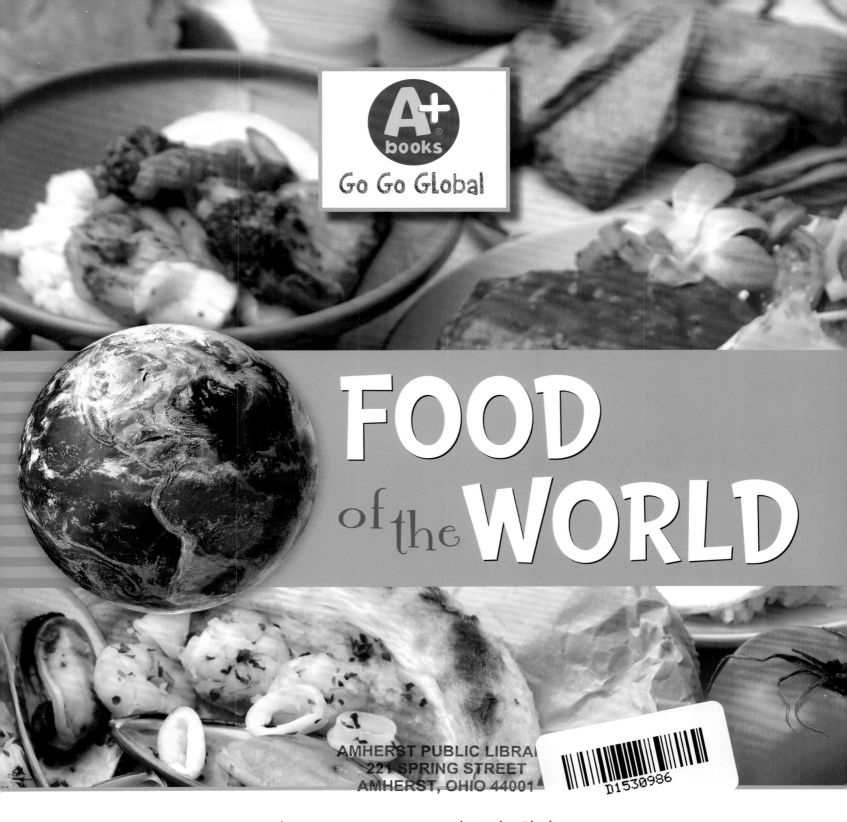

A+ books

Go Go Global

FOOD of the WORLD

by Nancy Loewen and Paula Skelley

CAPSTONE PRESS
a capstone imprint

Around the world, all the day through,

ice cream; United States

we lick and nibble, chomp and chew.

2

udon noodles; Japan

We **slurp** and
munch and
gobble too!

Morning's here, so open wide!

traditional breakfast; England

It's time to put some breakfast inside.

huevos rancheros; Mexico

Eggs or **porridge,**

rommegrot; Norway

spreads on **toast** ...

Vegemite spread; Australia

waffles

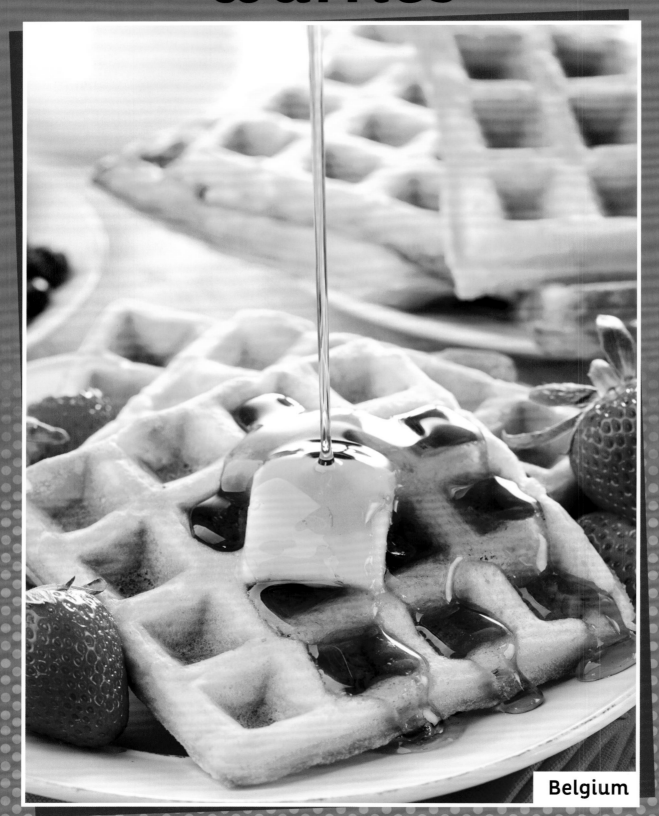

Belgium

or **falafel—**

Egypt

which do you like **most?**

What will **you** **munch** when it's **time** for **lunch?**

Thailand

Skewered meats in **spicy sauce,**

8

United States

ₐ **hot dog** in a **bun**...

empanadas,

Argentina

a **pizza slice** ...

Italy

munching lunch is **fun!**

Critters on sticks,

China

Australia

Colombia

Ireland

grubs, chocolate, and chips ...

snack
time
has us

spring rolls; Vietnam

Lady Finger bananas; Thailand

smacking our
lips.

tortilla chips and salsa; Mexico

The **day** has gone by.
It's **getting late.**

chicken and lamb curries; India

Time for **dinner—**
fill your **plate!**

aguadito; Peru

Sip some **soup** or **sample sushi.**

Japan

Bite a **burger** ...

United States

Morocco

or **kebab.**

Pass the **poutine**

Canada

and **paella.**

Spain

You **cleaned** your **plate**—
good job!

Holiday meals
set the mood.

roast turkey (for Thanksgiving); United States

Special days call for special **food.**

Donuts

fried and **filled** with **jam**,

tangyuan (for Winter Solstice Festival); China

sufganiyot (for Hanukkah); Israel

dumplings

soft and **tender**,

golden threads
of **sugar** and **egg**

foy thong cake (for weddings); Thailand

for **gatherings**
we'll **remember.**

Meat and corn steamed in leaves,

hallacas (for Christmas); Venezuela

"herring under a fur coat" (for New Year's Eve); Russia

fish topped off with veggies ...

a **pretty** pudding,

Christmas pudding (for Christmas); England

a tall ring cake—

food is how we celebrate.

kransekake (for weddings); Norway

27

Mmm … delicious.

Would you like more?

So many wonderful foods to explore!

chickpeas; Nigeria

layered rice cake with chicken; Iran

watermelon; Israel

beet soup; Ukraine

bird's nest baklava;
Turkey

meat and vegetables with flatbread; Ethiopia

29

NORTH
AMERICA

Canada

United
States

Mexico

SOUTH
AMERICA

Venezuela

Colombia

Peru

Argentina

EUROPE

Norway

Ireland
Belgium

England

Ukraine

Spain

Italy

Turkey

Morocco

Israel

Iran

Egypt

AFRICA

Nigeria

Ethiopia

ANTARCTICA

Russia

ASIA

China

Japan

India

Thailand —Vietnam

AUSTRALIA

Australia

GLOSSARY

celebrate—to do something fun on a special day

empanada (em-peh-NAH-deh)—a fried or baked pastry usually stuffed with meat

falafel (feh-LAH-fehl)—a spicy mixture of ground vegetables (such as chickpeas or fava beans) formed into balls or patties and then fried

grub—a soft, thick, wormlike larva of certain beetles and other insects

kebab (keh-BAHB)—cubes of meat cooked on a stick

paella (pah-AY-yeh)—a dish of rice, meat, seafood, and vegetables

porridge—a creamy, hot cereal

poutine (poo-TIN; poo-TEEN)—French fries topped with brown gravy and cheese

skewered—stuck on a stick

sushi (SOO-shee)—cold rice with raw seafood

CRITICAL THINKING USING THE COMMON CORE

1. Name three foods in this book that people around the world may eat for dinner. (Key Ideas and Details)

2. Look at the foods for special days. Explain how they are different from everyday foods. What makes them special? (Integration of Knowledge and Ideas)

A+ Books are published by Capstone Press,
1710 Roe Crest Drive, North Mankato, Minnesota 56003
www.capstonepub.com

Library of Congress Cataloging-in-Publication Data
Cataloging-in-publication information is on file with the Library
of Congress.
ISBN 978-1-4914-3918-0 (library binding)
ISBN 978-1-4914-3929-6 (paperback)
ISBN 978-1-4914-3939-5 (eBook PDF)

Editorial Credits
Jill Kalz, editor; Juliette Peters, designer; Tracy Cummins,
media researcher; Tori Abraham, production specialist

Photo Credits
Alamy: Gastromedia, 24; Shutterstock: Alex Hubenov, 14, Amornism,
Cover BR, baibaz, 4, Baloncici, 28 Top, Blend Images, 2, Bochkarev
Photography, 20, bonchan, 11, 17, Boris-B, 22 Left, Brent Hofacker, 6,
7, 18, cobraphotography, 5 TL, David P. Smith, 13 Bottom, deepblue-
photographer, 1, Dereje, 29 Bottom, dolphfyn, 22 Right, Dr Ajay Kumar
Singh, 28 BR, e2dan, 15 Top, gulserinak1955, 29 TL, HLPhoto, Cover
TL, 10, 19, 28 BL, jabiru, 5 Bottom, Jack.Q, 3, Karl Allgaeuer, Cover
TR, Cover BL, kavring, 5 TR, Kenneth Sponsler, 9, leocalvett, Cover,
1 (globe), Lesya Dolyuk, 26, Lisovskaya Natalia, 12 BR, m00osfoto, 12
Top, Olga Dmitrieva, 8, 16, Rakov Studio, 15 Bottom, senlektomyum,
13 Top, Settawat Udom, 13 Middle, skyfish, Cover Back, Stawek, 30
Bottom, Timolina, 25, topnatthapon, 23, V. Belov, 27, Vankad, 29 TR,
Zurijeta, 12 Middle; SuperStock: NHPA, 12 BL.

READ MORE

Bullard, Lisa. *My Food, Your Food.*
Alike and Different. Minneapolis:
Millbrook Press, 2015.

Curtis, Andrea. *What's for Lunch?:
How Schoolchildren Eat Around the
World.* Markham, Ontario, Canada:
Red Deer Press, 2012.

Menzel, Peter. *What the World Eats.*
Berkeley, Calif.: Tricycle Press, 2008.

INTERNET SITES

FactHound offers a safe, fun way to
find Internet sites related to this book.
All of the sites on FactHound have been
researched by our staff.

Here's all you do:
Visit *www.facthound.com*
Type in this code:
9781491439180

Check out projects, games and lots more at
www.capstonekids.com

Printed in China.
032015   008864WMF15

DEC   2015